How to Manage Remote Workers

Eryck Komlavi Dzotsi

Best Selling Author of The Remote Worker's Guide to Excellence

Printed in the United States of America

First Printing, 2014

ISBN-13: 978-1492956006

ISBN-10: 1492956007

Qomlavy Networks, llc
200 Umber ST NW
Palm Bay, FL 32907
+1-(321) 549-0886
www.qomlavy.com

Cover Design: Qomlavy Agency

Creative Consultant: E-Source Media

Publisher: Qomlavy Networks, LLC

Editor: Jenni Patel

DEDICATION

To
EJ Garcia (Esteban Juan Garcia IV)
who has been a sounding board, a frustration, a challenger, a supporter, a coworker, a teammate, a partner, but most importantly a friend for the last 10 years. Thanks for being a special case with all the good and bad. You sir, are a rock star and are one of the inspirations for this book.

George Francis Jr. and Joel Joseph
who believed in me before I even did in myself and equipped me in ways I can never repay them. Were I ever to be half the man you two cheer me on to be, I would have made it pretty big!

.

CONTENTS

ACKNOWLEDGMENTS

Thank you Jonathan Niebch for changing the course of my entire life... I'm forever indebted

Thanks Emily Gouwens, Katie Pasquinelli, and Melanie Kinney for showing me the way it ought to be done. The combination of the three of you is the best MBA School a professional can attend

Thank you Matt Naeger for taking me under your wing

Thank you Carissa Vega for being "my Village" throughout thick and thin. You are, and will always be the M to my James Bond

Thank you Ivan & Ashley Colaizzi for always making time

Thank you Jenni Patel for turning fiction into non-fiction and being the best non-wife a man could have

Thank you Jean Marc Mensah for being a friend-mentor

Thanks to Julian Anugom a.k.a Uncle J for blazing trails

Thank you Jim Foley for making lasting changes at Merkle

Thank you my small group, my family away from home

Thanks to Robert Lee, Stephanie Downs, Laurel Upton, Tony Hsieh, Clay Nichols, Jourdan Rombough, Zachary Simon, and Alexis Sanders for their input and illustrations

Thanks to all those not mentioned here; God bless you all

To Him in whom I find strength and satisfaction...

INTRODUCTION

I started working from home in March 2011 when I got a job in another state and was unable to sell my house in Florida. My new employer at the time gave me the opportunity to work from home in Melbourne instead of moving to Pittsburgh. I did some research online to understand how to best work from home and not betray the trust that my company had placed in me. I couldn't find good advice at the time, for the focus had been on how companies should approach working from home from an HR perspective. What there was about supporting remote workers didn't amount to much, and even less on how to motivate and make them successful.

I started jotting down all the mistakes I had committed during the transition. I stumbled quite a bit, but with every failure came a significant lesson. My manager would talk me through the mistakes I was making and would make suggestions on how to make improvements. I eventually applied the lessons, turned my performance around, and received praise from both clients and employers. I took all those heart felt lessons and wrote *"The Remote Worker's*

Guide to Excellence" which shot up to the top of Amazon's Best Sellers list a month after its publication. It still is today in the top 20 books in its category.

Excellence as a remote worker delivered nicely, for I was later promoted, and my perspectives and responsibilities changed. My new manager and my former managers came to life in my transition to the new role. Being an excellent remote worker was not enough, as the new challenge became how to motivate and manage other remote workers. The feedback I was getting from my readers became intense: now that you have taught us how to be a successful remote worker, you have to share with us your perspectives on how to assimilate, motivate and render productive remote workers under your management.

There are general guidelines on how to manage remote workers, but the key is that these general principles do not apply to A-players. I was now faced with the same realities that my readers were bringing up. I went back to the drawing board and started registering my mistakes, but this time around I also recorded the successes. Since I was managing what was probably the most astute team of SEO consultants in the US, and since many of those professionals were remote, my task was no longer to simply avoid the errors of the past, but to nail success down from beginning to end.

I tapped my fellow remote workers for their ongoing experiences and for what their managers could do more effectively. The abundance of feedback I received enabled me to view the common threads that tied all what I was hearing together. Even more significantly, I was also able to develop the awareness necessary to see the overarching pillars I subsequently worked with. When I was not managing a remote worker, I had meetings with other telecommuters, and the discussions would invariably turn to the challenges remotes were experiencing at the hands of managers in other organizations: disenchantment, disconnectedness and feelings of not belonging. This energized me endlessly and made me want all the more to come up with guiding principles leaders of virtual teams could benefit from wherever they are working.

Thus just like with my first book, this one is the results of conversations, research, opinion and analysis gathered over a couple of years from people on both sides of the management equation. As you will see, I have poured my heart and intellect into its various chapters, all to facilitate the task for anyone leading a team of workers in a remote environment.

Remote workers who excel at their job do not subscribe to some of the guidelines that office-based employees do. Those principles which may work on the average worker may very well hinder the development of the best performing remote workers. The key to the success of a manager of telecommuters is the ability to set the right boundaries of his/her resources and then unleash them. Nassirim Nyemebuio once told me that it is "the equivalent of being a racehorse jockey, where your purpose is to get the horse to feel relaxed and comfortable in the perfect lane, take him around masterfully, and then let him give it everything he's got to come first at the finish line."

My hope as you go through these pages is that you become a better leader of remote workers – that you learn how to get your team members to engage wholeheartedly with the team effort; to fit into the broader organization; to feel appreciated; to get relevant people at HQ to support you and be responsive to your team's needs; to be masterful at how you make yourself available. The anxiety of having people report to you from a distance as you await anxiously for their results is nothing compared to the reward you get as you see them elevate their personal development and productivity under your guidance.

This book applies primarily to managers who lead people working from home. The guiding principles apply to team members who work in a different office, on client locations or in other countries.

MY FIRST-HAND ENCOUNTER WITH GREATNESS

"One of the lessons of leadership worth emphasizing is that you want to get to know other great leaders and take their advice. At some point in your development, it's only people who've been in the seat of having to be leaders who can help you in a deep way." – Jim Yong Kim

A bowl of peach cobbler sat in front of me on this humid summer day, and my host looked at me over his own bowl and said "you are going to love it." He was right. That was the best peach cobbler I have tasted east of the Mississippi river. We were sitting on the back porch of a peaceful and very welcoming mid-20th century farmhouse in a borough of Pittsburgh, Pennsylvania. Except for the rackling noise of our spoons attacking the pie and ice cream in our bowls, only nature sounds filled the air. I looked at the three children surrounding me, I looked at the man to my right, and then across the table, I considered the lady that cooked our meal a few minutes before and made this succulent dessert from scratch... She is a Vice-President in the largest CRM agency in the United States, and she is a manager of remote workers. A stellar one. How in heaven and on earth does she pull this level of hospitality off after the day we have just had at the office?

This manager will remain unnamed because all of my attempts to reveal her identity have fallen on the sword of the humility with which she approaches many of her great achievements. On the day this dinner occurred, we have fought off several crisis on key strategic accounts where the resources responsible for the success of the work where spread to the four corners of the United States. The accounts managers were all remote employees. All meetings were held via conference calls, and many of the key instructions were given via IM, text messages and emails. Victory was achieved by all accounts at the end of the day, and what may have appeared like a unique set of circumstances were actually this manager's daily routine.

Some people who have complained about her management style during happy hours and other times of alcohol-induced boldness may challenge some of the assessments herein, but one thing that I have never heard anyone question is how great of a manager she is, whether you like her style or not. As business educators, we write books about management theories and their different applications and some other best practices. In some chapters, we will point to this or that individual as having some of the skills needed etc... But once in a while, as an educator of business professionals, you get the opportunity to point to someone and tell others "do what s/he does, and you will be just fine."

One might argue about her work-life balance and how insanely hard she works. One might even say that she may be a workaholic during certain periods of time, and her drive for excellence pushes her to work long hours. It is not surprising to see her online at 11:30pm several nights in a row. Of course I know this admittedly only because I am also online at those hours. She is not perfect by any stretch of the imagination, but her team performs excellently regardless of their geographical locations. When it comes to managing people, especially managing remote workers, this manager is the book example of how it ought to be done.

This book will go into details about traits and different types of acumen one can have, but let us walk through some examples of situations where all these elements come together for the benefits of the remote worker and by consequence, the benefit of the entire organization.

When she was promoted to VP of Client Services, a slew of "reply-all" emails ensued. People praising what a great example, mentor, manager etc... she has been. One email in particular caught the attention of many for being a bit excessive and brownnosing. A line in that email read "I would go to battle any day with you as a leader." Getting beyond what could be construed as ass-kissing by standing on the outside looking in, one may miss the fact that the author of the email is a lead account manager in the organization who not only is a remote worker but at the time was working on one of the most challenging yet profitable account of the organization. That account in four years has had many turn-overs at all levels may it director, managers, specialists, or strategists. One of the only few people that remained on the account and did so successfully by not only exceeding performance year over year but also earning the trust of the clients, did so while working from home and reporting to her.

In every war history, the victor has always been the one

whose presence remains with their troops long after their physical departure, and that ability to inspire towards performance without micromanagement is built on a trust edifice grounded on character and consistency. If you are a flake as a manager, your team will see it and will let you lead until a moment of crisis and you will be abandoned. People who work for her say of this manager "I feel like I can talk to her, and when I do, I trust what she is telling." You have to be able to inspire your team members near and far so that when they are left on their own to perform, they do so at optimum levels despite of challenges they could be faced with.

In the agency world, one goes from being a firefighter to being a plumber after being a circus juggler, right before being called on to save the world. For team members inside and outside of the office, it is a very stressful environment. Ignoring the challenges or wrapping them in a shroud of undervalue does not make them go away, and on the contrary, it sets the team members up for a great deal of disappointment and failure. A manager must be realistically optimistic as in they should maintain a positive attitude while acknowledging the painful and demanding nature of the work at hand. You will often hear her says "I know you are wondering how the hell you are going to do this, but you have what it takes. Trust me, I know it is not easy, but we can make it work."

Not being in the same room with your team creates communication challenges of their own. A great leader of remote employees ought to know how to lead the team through empowerment and delegation. One of the best instances of this challenge is the management of Astronauts in space from an earthly space base. Micromanaging is not an option. What are you going to do? Get on a plane and fly to the location of your employee and look over their shoulders? She syncs with her team before and after every major meeting or travel to clients sites to make sure that they have everything that they need She also debriefs them afterwards to give them an opportunity to air out any concern they have, and also to allow them to go through anything that they would like to change or maintain for the next performance. "I wanted to make sure, you have everything you need and that you are ready to go" is a statement which her team members are accustomed to. When expressed her team members know she means it. People around the office still tell the story about one remote worker who reported to her and traveled to a client location for a two-day trip where on the second day he was supposed to have a strategic meeting with the executives of this Fortune 500 Company. Weeks of preparation went into the trip. The remote worker gets to the client's office in Philadelphia and turns on his computer to be faced with "the blue screen of death." Upon being informed of the situation, this manager told the team member not to panic, and assured him that all will be in place for the meeting. She proceeded to escalate this situation in the organization. By the time the UPS trucked arrived for pick up at the office that day, a new laptop had been set and loaded with a mirror image of the remote worker's defunct computer, and a copy of the presentation was uploaded. When he showed up to client's office the next day, an overnight package delivery was awaiting him with all he needed. The meeting went well, and the company secured another success.

"I have been where you are right now, and I remember feeling like...." is a hard statement to make because many leaders focus on the stature and the position of leadership rather than focusing on the resources being led. This is a key danger for managers of in-office and the remote worker ones alike. You don't need to tell telecommuters the responsibility that comes with the privilege of working from home or elsewhere without being confined to a cube or office walls. Especially if you have a team of remote rock stars, understand that they self-assess on a daily basis and already beat themselves down for the task at hand.

Her team members have heard of her stories about her reply-all blunders and some of the challenges she was faced within her previous and current positions. The story of having to negotiate through a challenge issue with a client who pulled out a hunting knife and proceeded to sharpen it during their 1-on-1 meeting is my favorite. Humor bathed in empathy allows the leader of remote workers to take a great deal of weight off of their shoulders to allow them to perform their duties without that nagging feeling that not only they may screw up, but that they are faced with challenges no one would understand especially people in the office who have never seen these situations before.

The first time I heard this manager say "this one is on me," after we have been put in a difficult decision because of a decision she made, I wish I had a real universal remote controller so that I could rewind that moment and listen to it again. I was new to the organization, and I thought may be someone was playing a prank on me. Having worked my entire career in dog-eat-dog environments where people will throw each other under the bus constantly, I was in shock. A leader that takes responsibility demonstrates to the team of remote workers that the same level of accountability that is expected from them. That responsibility will be held up in the office as well. Being a remote worker makes you paranoiac, and if you subscribe to John Heller's "Just because you're paranoid doesn't mean they aren't after you," you have a hard time as it is all alone at home or in the field wondering how things are in the office and under what bus you are about to be thrown. A leader of remote workers must extract that fear from her team members, and in some occasions fall on the sword for her team in order to allow them to move forward for the sake of the entire organization.

On dark days where the team members were stressed, and platitude smeared with frustration, it is the routine to see a particular project through completion, team members get pushed to their limits. People in the office settings will vent to one another, but after the team gets off the phone or the conference call, the remote workers are left to commiserate by themselves. Over the years talking to remote workers, one thing you hear often, is "I just got off the phone with her, and I leveled with her. It is was really good that she reached out when she did." This manager always made sure to reach out to her remote team members to break the wall of isolation.

In the middle of conflicts where some of the team members are remote and some are in an office settings, the communication is not always the best. In the fall of 2013, account management team members who are remote where locked in a grueling argument with the analytics team members who were in the office. Things got really heated, and then this manager stepped in, calmed everyone down, gave a voice to the remote workers, and then played the role of Porte-parole for the in-office team members; she ended by saying another one of her famous crisis-adverting statements she is known for "how about we do this....." Having a great deal of intuition to be aware of what the team members need and when they need them will position a manager of remote workers to be able to offer timely support to her team. Catering the ability to be a great decision maker who does not play favorites but offers a path towards resolution will make a leader earn the respect and commitment of remote workers because even when they disagree with the decision, they trust the decision maker for her proven ability and past results.

She often goes out of her way to call, text, IM her team members to make sure of their wellbeing professionally and personally. It is not a surprise when her team members are either sick or dealing with issues to see her reach out to them to see how she and the organization can help. The key is not just going through the motion of caring, but a manager who genuinely cares about his/her team members will earn the respect and the admiration of the latters. Caring without being weak is a balance, you can see that this manager is never disrespected by the people who work for her.

Lastly but almost even more importantly is the fact that reading the above, some may think that she is a nice and soft leader, but that would be a mistake. As enjoyable as it is having this manager in your corner, it is an equally growing experience than to be on her disciplinary side. Her care does not prevent her from keeping her team accountable and to deal with them factually and sternly when needed. There is no sugar-coating, but a great deal of understanding is demonstrated to her team. She holds her team accountable to clear performance goals and will take actions to help you improve or pay the consequences of your lack of performance. She communicates to her team that mistakes happen and are to be expected, but it does not make them right or negligible. From mistakes, lessons should be learned, and the re-occurrence should be avoided; she will make sure that you get that message. Strict discipline applied through the filter of care and empathy allows honesty to fly both ways in the manager-resource relationship.

Malcolm Gladwell is one of my literary heroes, and from him I learned that it is easier to explain a concept by using someone who personifies it rather than simply engaging in a litany of theories. When it comes to managing remote workers, this is the way to do it. As you read through the rest of the book, keep this chapter in mind, and you will start to identify the key concepts illustrated in the preceding words.

_2_
YAHOO! IS NOT THE RULE

"Nature provides exceptions to every rule." – Margaret Fuller

"Systems are to be appreciated by their general effects, and not by particular exceptions." – James F. Cooper

On July 16, 2012, Marissa Mayer was selected President and Chief Executive Officer of Yahoo! In 2013, Mayer was ranked 32 in Forbes Magazine's report of the World's 100 Most Powerful Women. That same year, Mayer was the first lady mentioned on the top of the Fortune magazine's annual report of the best 40 business stars under 40 years old. In 2014, she was mentioned once again on the list of 100 most powerful females worldwide. She was positioned at number eighteen, right after Beyoncé Knowles. To say that Marissa Mayer was a rock star among Tech CEOs would be an understatement. She took the reins of flailing Yahoo! and quickly set out to make an impact. She changed the logo, made some strategic acquisitions and managed to reinvigorate the investors, driving Yahoo! stock prices up for the first time in recent memories. She was on a roll. Marissa Mayer's modifications to Yahoo! were however not all accepted positively.

In February 2013, Mayer started a workforce policy change that required all remote-working staff to become in-office staff. Jackie Reses, Yahoo's executive vice president of people and development, delivered a memo asking remote workers to make their way to the company's offices. Yahoo's 14,500 remoter workers had until June of that year to get into the office setting — if not, they may be fired.

On February 22, 2013, AllThingsD posted a leaked version of a Yahoo memo by their head of Human Resources, Jackie Reses, that announced, "we have to be one Yahoo!, and that begins with physically being together."

Another part of the memo read:

"Beginning in June, we're asking all employees with work-from-home arrangements to work in Yahoo! offices. If this impacts you, your management has already been in touch with next steps. And, for the rest of us who occasionally have to stay home for the cable guy, please use your best judgment in the spirit of collaboration. Being a Yahoo isn't just about your day-to-day job, it is about the interactions and experiences that are only possible in our offices."

Reses wields the carrot and the stick in her declaration for the new work-at-Yahoo's-office strategy. The claim is that telecommuting decreases Yahoo! synergy and reduces the quality of its services. As stated by Reses, "Speed and quality are often sacrificed when we work from home." It's not a secret that Yahoo! was floundering in recent years and was dwarfed by the growth of its competitor Google. Yahoo! was rapidly losing ground in the online advertising and marketing arenas. In fact, it outsourced it search operations to Bing. Something needed to be done. Was getting rid of remote workers the answer? "Some of the best decisions and insights come from hallway and cafeteria discussions, meeting new people, and important team meetings" claimed the memo contending that in-person conferences increased the quality of strategic choices and business ideas.

Innovation is cited as one of the root for the decision that was made. Google is full of super-smart engineers who come up with new businesses and ideas that help it to improve its bottom line. New business strategies emerge when smart and wise people from various professions get together to interact around common goals and concepts, independently of their physical locations. Google however enables its workers to work at home on a case-by-case according to an article in the New York Times. Yet it does not seem to be marred by the problems Marissa Meyer is solving by sending the employees back into the office. Where Google is often cited in conversations evolving around innovation, rarely is this the case for Yahoo! There is a fundamental difference in these companies approach to innovation. Marissa Mayer's former employer, Google, did not have an efficiency problem. Google's 53,861 employees produce $931,657 in profits per worker, which was at the time 170% greater compared to Yahoo's $344,758 in profits per employee.

But Yahoo! was claiming otherwise.

"To become the absolute best place to work, communication and collaboration will be important, so we need to be working side-by-side. That is why it is critical that we are all present in our offices. Some of the best decisions and insights come from hallway and cafeteria discussions, meeting new people, and impromptu team meetings. Speed and quality are often sacrificed when we work from home. We need to

be one Yahoo!, and that starts with physically being together."

Certainly, it's understandable why Mayer would lean in this direction, and her reasoning behind this decision is sound. Yes, there are people who abuse the privilege of telecommuting. Yes, telecommuting is not for everyone. Yes, there often is no substitute for in-person, face-to-face interactions. And yes, Yahoo!'s workforce – and every workforce – needs to be more disciplined to get and stay ahead in a competitive world.

Telecommuting Can Work for Employers & Employees

I understand Mayer's decision. However, I respectfully disagree with her. My experience as a telecommuter, and the experience of thousands of telecommuters around the nation, is living proof that telecommuting works, and both employees and the organizations that employ them can benefit.

Employees benefit from greater flexibility, less stress, saving money on expenses like gas, parking and tolls, and fewer hassles and distractions, which ultimately leads to greater productivity. Employers benefit, too, because telecommuting attracts top talent, saves money on office space, and yes, more engaged, productive, and happy employees – and there's evidence this is true.

According to a study by Cisco, approximately sixty-nine percent of the employees surveyed cited higher productivity when working remotely, and seventy-five percent of those surveyed said the timeliness of their work improved. Eight-Three percent of employees said their ability to communicate and collaborate with co-workers was the same as, if not better than, it was when working onsite. Sixty-Seven percent of employees said their overall work quality improved when telecommuting. More than Ninety-one percent of respondents say telecommuting is somewhat or very important to their overall satisfaction.

Don't Eliminate Telecommuting – Improve It

Despite the benefits of telecommuting, there are still pitfalls. Yahoo! and other companies still have qualms about telecommuting. That doesn't mean telecommuting should be eliminated, but rather that employers need to make sure they provide the right conditions for employees to succeed as telecommuters, and employees need to determine if telecommuting is right for them.

Set and manage clear expectations.

Employers and employees enter into telecommuting arrangements with certain expectations, which can lead to problems if not met. Both parties need to determine if telecommuting makes sense for employees, their managers, and the company as a whole, and then define and communicate their expectations with respect to productivity, work hours and access to company resources.

Ultimately, business is about results. As a CEO, Mayer should understand that what matters is not where her employees work, but how they work, what they accomplish, and why they need to accomplish what they do. Consider the fact that an individual whose job it is to fix a technical problem with Yahoo! Mail doesn't necessarily develop new business suggestions. She may come up with a new way to fix the code behind the mailing system. Whether this person works at home or in an office with other people, should anyone really care as long as the email system works efficiently?

Do not let Yahoo! deter you from seeing remote working as a viable and successful option for your business. According to the National Study of Employers, 63% of companies in 2012 allowed employees to work some hours from home compared with 34 percent in 2005. In a recent

Reuters article on the subject, you can learn that Aetna's CEO Mark Bertolini and national business chief Joseph Zubretsky have shared in numerous occasions that 14,500 of the 35,000 Aetna's employees do not have a desk at Aetna which resulted in the company cutting 2.7 million square feet of office space at $29 a square foot, for about $78 million in cost savings a year.

_3_
HOW TO HIRE ELITE REMOTE WORKERS

"I am convinced that nothing we do is more important than hiring and developing people. At the end of the day you bet on people, not on strategies." – Lawrence Bossidy, GE

"If you pick the right people and give them the opportunity to spread their wings and put compensation as a carrier behind it, you almost don't have to manage them." – Jack Welch

Remote workers are those employees who perform their duties from home or those who are working from a location other than their home office either while travelling for business on behalf of their organization, or from a facility other than where their manager or hierarchical authorities are located. Telecommuters are becoming more common today and the trend is growing as more and more people are able to arrange their work hours around challenges such as distance from the office or competing in markets that are different than the location where the company is headquartered.

Some have predicted that remote workers will be a growing trend in the future and other groups are not considering them as a quick replacement for traditional onsite working arrangements. At present times, remote workers are growing in numbers and though companies such as Yahoo! have made headline by sending all the remote workers back in house, current hiring trends suggest that it had had little impact on the growth of remote workers hiring.

The main challenge in managing remote workers start at the resource acquisition level. If you hire people who are incapable of working remotely, it does not matter how great of a manager you are, your team and organization will either fail or spend resources fixing a problem it should have avoided altogether. The main key ingredient is to hire motivated, efficient and talented remote workers to achieve high productivity. As many in-office unproductive workers do after joining organization, the remote workers ones will also disappear without proper tracking and you will not find out until it is too late. This is more dangerous if you are filling critical positions with remote team members. If you hire the wrong people and send them to work from home, don't be surprised by the results. The wrong resources placed in a role that they are neither prepared for nor are competent to succeed in is a formula for unrecoverable disaster.

It is a simple fact that is however overlooked by so many companies. The error is made in the recruitment process itself. Companies seek out local candidates, when they do not find them, they then expand the geographical limits of the search area with the purpose of relocating the potential candidate. When the relocation is not an option based on the importance of the role to be filled, the organization then looks at remote options. The job offer or the interview processes are not updated when this shift in prerogatives occurs, and therefore many well intended hiring managers end up hiring resources that would have excelled in an in-office environment and place them in a remote condition. No matter how great of a manager you are, if your team members that you hire are not adequately equipped to work from home, you will fail as their manager, and your entire team will come down crumbling.

Are there employee qualities that make someone a better candidate for remote work? Absolutely. If the employee has never worked for your organization, you would like to be on the lookout for individuals who are highly experienced in the field selected. The level of independence required to succeed as a remote worker makes it that having a non-experienced individual placed in that role will necessitate attention and growth that the organization and the manager cannot often afford to put in place. This is even more important in an agency or consulting firm because the remote employees on top of being in other locations are often on client sites or on the battle field being required to make decisions in the moment. These decisions are the ones that the whole organization will have to deliver upon or fully support. Hiring effective and excellence-prone remote workers while eliminating candidates from the unproductive pool of applicants is the equivalent of a jigsaw puzzle. The resume of a potential candidate may position them to seem to you that they will be thriving outside of a home-office environment but this alone is a poor indicator of their ability to excel and you will never know what will be the other side of the picture. How do you then nail the recruitment?

The Job Post

The first piece of the puzzle is to place an advertisement which clearly states you are hiring remote workers on job banks and recruiting websites, social media platforms, newspapers or any other medium where you intend to recruit your remote workers. You don't have to mention items such as working from home arrangements, but you should emphasize the importance of the ability to perform duties from remote sites, client locations, and other locations with limited supervisions. The advertisement should mention clear, accurate and informative job description and job specification which portrays your organization's requirement. If a candidate shows up to an interview and did not realize it was a position for a remote worker, that candidate should be out of the pool right away. People who do not meet the above mentioned criteria should be rejected. A clear job description eliminates unproductive workers from the list and makes it easy for organizations to fine-tune the screening process.

The Screening

The next step towards hiring efficient remote workers is adopting a systematic screening process. After accepting the applications, every resume will be passed through a three-step categorization-screening process. This will take out most unqualified applications from the pool for further progress. You should first review the applications which contain people which are the most qualified for the job. Secondly you will prioritize the applicants with experience working from home or away from the office. The third key elements will be to look in the work history for positions that required a lot of in-the-moment decision making and self-starting qualities. The resulting candidates should be given a test/problem/scenario to work through and complete within a tight deadline in order to disqualify any potential frauds early on before going to the next round. Through this test you are trying to assess their competence fit, not their social one. Train your staff to look for the levels of creativity, productivity, efficiency and knowledge.

The Interview Process

The interview process should have multiple elements of the remote working reality such as:

• a phone interview where the candidate will have to solve a problem verbally without any visual support.

• a video interview (Skype, Lync, etc...) to gauge the candidate's ability to perform on videoconferences.

• an in-person interview where part of the audience is in the room and the other part dialed into the phone. Analyze the candidate closely during the in-person interview. Understand that any perceived mistake could be exacerbated once they are on their own.

What qualities are you looking for during the interview?
• Drive and passion
• Self-sufficiency and self-motivation
• Excellent project management skills
• Good communication skills
• Organizational and operational skills
• Technological savvy
• Focus and prioritization acumen

Make sure no matter how much you are impressed by a specific candidate you conduct a thorough cross-referencing so you are provided with extra dimensional views about the candidates. Though this seems like a complex endeavor, organizations have to make sure the time-consumed in hiring the most talented and reliable remote workers will reduce their risk of being disappointed and have to search for new remote workers in the future.

Get close and get to know them

Know what makes the candidates feel validated:
- Compensation (Money)
- Benefits
- Work-Life balance
- Praise and Recognition
- Development and Career Opportunities
- Making a Difference

Whatever the answer is, make sure you deliver upon it. If you find that they derive satisfaction through money, make sure in your negotiations the compensation you give them at least meets their expectations. You do not want them to be on a tough day at home, working on very challenging projects, and all that they can think about is that they wish they were making more money than you currently are giving them. If recognition and praise motivate them, make sure you communicate with them manager to understand how they like feedback to be given.

Once you reach a mutual agreement and a start date is selected, make sure you prepare, for yourself, a plan to manage through the initial stages of their employment and execute your plan.

Allow for a trial period.

As mentioned earlier, telecommuting is not for everyone. Allow a trial period; for example, 90 days, to uncover if the telecommuting arrangement makes the most sense for you and your employees. At the end of the trial period, you can either allow employees to continue telecommuting or require them to work in the office, depending on how well things went during that time.

Train telecommuters properly.

Telecommuters have unique knowledge needs for everything from how to log into the company network and set up teleconferences to how to communicate with a geographically dispersed team. The right training, or lack thereof, can mean the difference between success and contentment or failure and frustration. Do not rely on the training as a crutch for your poor recruiting decision.

Zach Simon, a Delivery Lead in Digital Marketing who not only works from home but also manages many remote employees explained to me that "*It is very tough to train new people that have little skill, much easier to have more tenured staff work from home. Training someone from a distance is extremely difficult and truly gauging someone's passion for the work that they need to do, not just having a job, is very difficult when you are teaching them the job remotely.*"

Provide opportunities for in-person socialization.

Many remote workers feel "out of the loop" when it comes to the goings-on in the office, and the folks in the office feel the same way about their telecommuting peers. Inviting your telecommuting employees to onsite social functions, whether at the home office or satellite locations, gives you a chance to get to know telecommuters as people and see the faces behind the screen.

Set up a structure for accountability.

People work harder and accomplish more when they feel accountable. A telecommuting arrangement should provide a solid structure for accountability, whether it involves weekly status reports or quarterly onsite one-on-one sessions.

If you are hiring a manager that will have responsibilities over remote employees, you want to also be on the lookout for key elements. Good candidates are managers who are:

- Highly organized and disciplined
- Excellent communicators
- Empathetic
- Patient.
- Committed to the success of the remote employee
- Able to manage by results; not by observation
- Comfortable with delegating tasks and responsibilities – clear and complete instructions – checks for understanding and agreement
- Prone to provide appropriate and timely feedback

If your company does not currently have remote employees, and you are reading this book to find answers on how to make sure you launch a successful remote program, this hiring step is going to be your most important one. If you recruit the right resource, you will be able to not only quickly ramp up your team expansions, but you will have a live example within your organization to showcase the value of remote workers and their ability to succeed if given the right resources.

Zach Simon also shared with me his experience with an exceptional remote worker whom for privacy reasons would be named Xavier. At the time Zach was working in a company office in Pittsburgh and the company did not have many remote workers and considered the option with a dose of apprehension.

"When Xavier and I began working together I was hesitant to think that working remotely would be something that could easily fit into our office culture. Xavier rapidly came up to speed on our accounts and the way we do business, quickly proving my instinct wrong. While working from home, Xavier has found clever ways to keep communication open, make sure that he, nor

anyone remote, is forgotten or doesn't have a spot at the table, and ultimately make sure that remote employees not only survive, but thrive. His success as a remote employee laid the groundwork for our organization to reconsider our footprint for hiring which was holding us back. I couldn't be more appreciative for the role he played when I needed to move closer to family yet, loved my job and wanted to stick with our company."

Now that we have identified the elements necessary to recruit and onboard a remote worker/manager. What are now the elements that allow you as the manager to succeed?

_4_
LEADERSHIP AS A MATTER OF CHARACTER

"A leader is one who knows the way, goes the way, and shows the way." John C. Maxwell

"A leader is best when people barely know he exists, when his work is done, his aim fulfilled, they will say: we did it ourselves." Lao Tzu

In August of 1940, at the height of WWII, and when the British Air Force won the decisive "battle of the air", the British Prime Minister and leader, Winston Churchill, said this in a famous speech: "Never in the field of human conflict was so much owed by so many to so few." He was expressing gratitude to the air force but, more significantly, motivating his nation and his entire armed forces –most of whom were in faraway battlefields. Many of the military leaders have met him once, yet once they were in the battlefield away from the homeland and the military headquarters, they carried out their duties with excellence and honors.

The soldiers who were fighting in cold and unwelcoming ditches in faraway places felt gratified by their leader's words. Why? Because they knew he was sincere, that he felt for them, and that he was doing his best on their behalf. If one is going to exert influence from a distance, those caught in the faraway sphere of influence have to feel the authenticity and the high moral ground of the speaker and leader. You can't be known as an exaggerator, embellisher, or occasional fibber and exert such influence.

We humans are constantly influencing one another. It has been said you influence at least 10,000 people during your lifetime – even if you are a great introvert. Sometimes we influence one another simply because we are too lazy or uncertain in our beliefs to make a decision on our own. That, by the way, is one of the reasons why the concept of 'reviews" flourished so much of late. We need to see what other people thought in order to validate our own thinking. In this context, the person who leaves the review is the one who exerts the influence – in an entirely remote fashion.

"Influencing" is less demanding than "leading". We influence each other through a variety of factors: our body language, voice, the way we gaze at people, the clarity of what we say, our integrity, the clothes we wear, and so on. If, for example, you are completely uncertain as to what clothes to wear, and one of your friends is always dressed stylishly, you would naturally gravitate towards that person's sphere of influence. Similarly, he who speaks clearly and with a booming voice has enormous appeal.

Leaders however have attributes that go beyond their mere presence and manners. They have stature, an ability to project their leadership to places far beyond their communities or network of followers and, most importantly, they have one or more messages that resonate widely with followers.

How does one lead a team without being present?

Leaders first attract, then they persuade, and finally they exert their influence. To influence people around them, it helps if they have a whole array of qualities. Listed here are four of the most important qualities:

1. They must be outgoing individuals who exude the virtues of love, compassion and empathy. The dictionary defines empathy as "the capacity to recognize emotions that are being experienced by another being." Empathy is the precursor to love and compassion, and a great speaker has genuine empathy for every person in his or her community, as well as remotely.

2. A great leader is also a highly intuitive person, much like a creative business manager or inventor. To understand what is meant by "intuitive", think of Bill Gates during the process of creating Microsoft. He and his top team would not get bogged down in every detail but, instead, imagine them up in a hot air balloon looking down not only at the current developments, but at the outcomes that have not yet been thought of.

3. An intuitive department head knows instinctively what task to assign to each of his or her employees, and who among them needs more assistance than others. This is not always a question of past delegating experience, because some of the assigned tasks may never have come up in the past. It is a mix of experience plus a hefty dose of instinct. After all, the department head did not get to that position purely because of his or her experience. They got there because they also showed promise – to their intuitive

leadership team.

4. Leaders with a net of followers that extends well past their immediate communities are optimists at heart. After a talk or speech, they can be counted upon to leave their audience with an elevated spirit, looking forward.

Every part of the above applies to the business manager who, for example, has 40 employees in the US and 25 in Hong Kong.

The staff in Hong Kong have to know, if the manager is effective, that he or she cares for them, that they are a part of the US team, that their interests are uppermost on the manager's mind and –again- that the manager has high moral standing, is competent and, generally speaking, a person to be admired in every sense of the word.

To be in a managerial position and inspire and influence others – or to be a high ranking officer in the armed forced- is in itself a level of achievement that puts you squarely on the road to becoming a significant player in any field of your choice. The residual benefits of attaining the status of a "leader of remote teams" in fact extends to fairly every other part of your life: you boost your self-confidence to new heights; you become more credible and persuasive; you get recognized and are treated as an expert at what you do; your interpersonal skills get honed, enabling you to win people over; you become a great listener; you get to deal with difficult people more adroitly; you learn to speak clearly and with a voice that resonates; and you get to champion any cause of your choice, moving it forward effectively.

Clayton Nichols, a successful account manager for the largest Customer Relationship Management (CRM) Agency in the US who is known not just for his understanding of Search Engine Optimization but also his ability to deliver results on complex e-commerce projects completed the merger of two companies who then became the fifth largest e-commerce platform in North America. He worked for extended amount of time on client locations and reported to a manager who was also a remote worker. He described his experience as follows:

"When I was first hired to my agency, my new boss helped me easily transition to the new fast-paced world, but the key thing was that he was not in our office. He was a remote worker who was managing a team that was in different locations. While it can be difficult at times to display emotion or the ability to care through an instant message or a phone call, if you make sure to consistently set the right tone through voice and video communications, that trust between employee and manager can easily grow and the character of the persons involved can shine through. My manager has always displayed the ability to show compassion and understanding while being hundreds of miles away, to his credit, he's always made himself available and open when necessary and that helps establish, in everyone else's mind that he is reliable, trustworthy, and able to perform his job above expectations. Those experiences of always being able to handle a problem or making sure to be available when it's needed the most has been absolutely crucial in my ability to perform through stressful moments and being remote simply isn't an issue."

Our character is one of the components of our performance that is not only difficult to hide from others, but it plays a crucial role in our ability to lead and empower others.

_5_
CHALLENGES TO MANAGING REMOTE TEAMS

"When a management with a reputation for brilliance tackles a business with a reputation for bad economics, it is the reputation of the business that remains intact." - Warren Buffett

As Yahoo!'s example demonstrates, there are many challenges that come with managing remote workers. Our objective here is not to portray the contrary. These challenges range from the most common to the most disastrous set of circumstances. Robert Lee, Founder and Partner at Circa Interactive, a Marketing Agency specializing in Higher Education, shared one of those with me in their office in San Diego, CA.

"With a wide array of thirsty and highly talented contractors available across the globe, it makes complete business sense to delve into the possibility of finding a cheaper but fully qualified remote worker from another country. Using these workers has

enabled us to offer our services at a cheaper rate to our clients, while still paying our contractors a wage that is highly competitive in their local areas. With that being said, the realities of the world come into play when a worker cannot meet a deadline due to an unforeseen disaster, take for example, the 2014 typhoon in the Philippines. Our contractor, whom we have built a strong personal and professional relationship with over the last three years, was for the most part unaffected by the disaster, but his country was not. All power and forms of communication were down for weeks, which obviously created a large problem when it came to deadlines. While we understood the issue, our team is based in San Diego, and our client had a hard time understanding why we were late on the project. All in all this was a great learning experience for our business when it came to international contractors… be ready for the unexpected. While everything might be humming along status quo within our local area, other societies around the world do not have the luxuries when it comes to infrastructure which we take for granted. Things were eventually able to get back to normal for our contractor and we have continued our fantastic relationship, but since then we have introduced backup procedures so our organization can still produce results even when unforeseen events arise."

As Circa Interactive's experience clearly demonstrates, having remote workers means you will have to deal with issues your main office is not dealing with. When all the team members are under your roof, your emergency and operating procedures for that location would cover most of the issues that can arise, not so when your other team members are not covered by those rules. In successfully managing remote workers, a great deal of flexibility is therefore required.

Many of the challenges mainly affect the remote worker and do not directly affect you as their manager. Your ability to deal with that challenge for and with them will ensure their success and therefore your own. For many remotes, being away from the office is great because working from home or in a different location is giving them a feeling they can manage their own time, working whenever and wherever they want. The benefits often hide many disadvantages from this work which can lead the team members to quit in order to revert to having normal working settings in the company or at another institution.

The (Not So) Great Escape and Need for Boundaries
When you work in an office, the culture of the environment, the social queues, and other dynamics allow you to build a structure where often external elements are the safeguard to production and efficiency. Some employees may not be distracted by events and people at an office, but when they work at home then they will become responsible for all the queues and production gatekeeping that is available otherwise. One of the greatest challenge is the notion that when you are at home, it is very easy to find a chore you have to do because whatever you were supposed to be working on could wait since you can do it later (though this is the priority that should be attributed to the said chore).

Jourdan Rombough, an SEO Account Manager in New York often works from home. He shared with me the importance of establishing boundaries.

> *"My mother and sister came to visit me for a week and I naturally let them stay at my place. They were excited that I had the ability to work from home so they could see more of me. However, I should have communicated that they needed to consider me as unavailable, as though I were at the office. I did not realize how tempting it was for them to ask me for favors or quickly chat it up as long as I didn't look busy – the situation was a disaster waiting to happen.*

It even went so far that my sister asked me to run a 10 minute errand for her. My subtle hints unfortunately did not sink in when I mentioned how extremely busy I am, or how important it is that I need to focus. I had to sit them down to clearly set up boundaries and expectations. I explained that, unless it is an emergency, they need to have it in their minds that I am not here. My mother and sister were very understanding when I finally set this expectation. My kind, loving sister told me she needs to remember that even though I look like a complete slob at my computer, I am still doing important work (that's genuine sibling love for you). Minimizing unnecessary distractions like these from your day will make all of the difference when you are working remotely in the presence of company."

Boundaries need to be set and are the sole responsibility of the remote worker. You need to challenge the remote worker to establish these very early on. For more junior team members, you should go the distance of reviewing those boundaries with them periodically. For many people, the office is often an escape from the troubles at home. The reality is our home lives are not always perfect. Whether you live at home with your parents, with friends, as a couple, or with kids, there are always challenges that often arise. Working from home takes away that escape opportunity in some way. If you are going through a foreclosure/divorce/illness/name your obstacle, it can be challenging to be in the house by yourself (or with others) and not think about these things. Other things such as laundry, home deliveries, and needed errands can constitute additional major distractions. Your team members' ability to draw boundaries between their work hours and their home hours will allow them to overcome this challenge.

What is the big deal with Balance?

Many articles and blog posts have been written about the

notion of work-life balance and how important it is. Many managers often tell their employees about the need to strike a proper balance in their lives. We need, as managers, to understand the elusive nature of that concept. Remote employees should not stop working long hours just because they are told to or because others do. The reverse is also true in that they should work more hours just because others do. It's all about balance. My scale is not your scale and there aren't always standards. Suppose your company may have a requirement for you to work an average of 45 hours per week. If you sleep 7 hours a night, that leaves you with 74 hours of life as there are 168 hours in a calendar week (120 hours in a work week). Some people might say that 74 hours (or 40 hours per work week) is more life than work, and some may disagree. If you count the sleep time as part of your life time, the balance tips even more. It is therefore fundamental you let your remote team members define for themselves what constitutes balance. It will depend on where they are in their life cycle.

Balance for a 22-year old out of college single woman with no kids is not the same as that of a 46-year old executive who is a mother of three kids and has to take care of sick parents. For some people 40 hours per week is enough. For some others 65 hours is more like the norm. Whichever is best for your remote team members and acceptable to your company should be the target for which you strive as a team. Do not adopt or do not force your remote team members to adopt someone else's definition of work-life balance, as this is a sure formula towards disaster.

The other reason why you need, as a manager, to have a conversation with your resources on a frequent basis about balance is that though they cherish it, most remote workers don't track their balance but rather the work that needs to get done. As Zachary Simon puts it *"I wind up working a lot more."* It is quite an interesting dynamic that occurs. People who work from home do not have a need for things like "beating the traffic" or "running out to get lunch," so more available time gets added up to what they would normally consider as part of their work time. Very few people reallocate that gained time to life activities, but rather leverage it to get more things done "at work."

Recommend to your employees that they schedule post-work activities that require them to get out of the house. I myself take ballroom dancing classes or meet with a personal trainer during the week. Since I have already paid for those classes, I am incentivized not to miss them. Tony Hsieh, a fellow remote worker who is also an SEO rock star shared with me his experience.

> *"When I became a remote worker, one of the first things I did was to join local meet-up groups. I would recommend this. It doesn't really matter what groups I joined. People should pick something that interests them. There are numerous types of groups, so just pick one that interests you. Each group has its own objective so mix and match business with social, or technical with outdoor meetup groups. It is one way to meet interesting people. One of the groups I joined was a "Work from home" group that meet bi-weekly for lunch. It's basically people who work from home and who gather once in a while to talk about….. whatever we feel like talking about."*

The old Communication problem

This is another problem companies have to face, even if remote workers have the same native language as you. There can be trouble with giving instructions if you have to do it over the phone or over emails and IMs. When communication occurs via emails, instant messages, or text, explanations can be misunderstood. In-person interactions, or through video conferencing, with employees allows you to clarify and give further detailed information. As a manager of remote workers, you have to take it upon yourself to ensure there are no misunderstandings. Recapping instructions and following up on directives to make sure clarity is achieved must be pursued especially at the onset of the working relationship. The added effort in establishing communications patterns, very early on, will benefit the team in the long run.

Communication strains can be amplified if you are hiring in a different culture. When a company decides to hire a remote worker whose native language is not native to that of the country in which the main office is located, one should expect a few challenges when it comes to translating instructions for projects. Although remote workers may understand the same language (you hired them for their ability to perform the work in your language right) they could not completely grasp the complexities of industry-specific business jargon.

Engagement

We have an entire chapter dedicated to the engagement element, but I wanted to introduce the subject here due to its important. You run a team as a manager, and regardless of their physical locations, it is important all your team members feel like they indeed are part of the team. Most remote workers to whom we have spoken in our research complained about feeling disconnected. The sense of belonging or the notion of "drinking the company cool aid" are rendered difficult in this working environment. It is difficult for your remote team to learn about your company culture, and it is even more difficult for them to have learning opportunities beyond their immediate job. As a result, you end up with employees who have a hard time feeling part of the team because of the lower quality relationship that they are nurturing with co-workers. As you know, getting things done around the office requires often that you ask assistance from people who are not part of your day-to-day operating routines. You do this by either walking into their office or crossing their paths in the building. That subtle yet important aspect of being in an office environment is taken away from your remote working teams. This could result in frustration with getting things done, and more importantly a very low alignment with your company culture. Remote employees therefore lack the same level of buy-in as in-office employees. While it's possible to find a worker who's as dedicated to the vision as you are, it's much more likely you'll have to work hard to get their commitment. You have to make it your objective as a manager of remote workers that you have to do this on a short-term basis and on a on a per-project basis. Never take the commitment of a remote worker for granted and avoid to nurture it. You'll otherwise encounter a higher turnover and training costs.

When dealing with the issues remote workers are faced with, it is important not to just focus on those. You don't have to remind them of the benefits, but you should be conscious of the fact that working from home is not all that bad.

Office Space? No Thanks

The first benefit is that they get to work in an environment they have a complete control over. This new-found control allows them to dictate things like where they work, what they wear, how they decorate, what music they listen to and how loudly, how late to work etc…

Saving Time, Money, and Hassle

They save the time that they would have spent otherwise commuting in and out of the office. People in major urban areas will greatly value this benefit. Gone are the stressful traffic jams and long train/bus rides.

Less traffic and air pollution
To your environmentally conscious employees the notion that their ability to drive less is contributing to improving the environment by producing less toxic air.

_6_
IF YOU SUCK AS A MANAGER, THIS WILL MAKE IT WORSE

"Nobody works better under pressure. They just work faster." — *Brian Tracy*

"Pressure is something you feel when you don't know what the hell you're doing." Peyton Manning

Countless books have been written on the subject of Management. A search on Amazon.com for "management" returns 953,933 results for Books. The scientific art of business and people management has existed from the very first there has been more than one human being on the face of the earth. Yet it's mastery is still a sign of great awe. When in our career, we get to work for a great manager, we cherish it. Of all the things taken for granted, having a great manager is not one. According to Wilson Learning research on employee engagement, happiness at work is the direct result of the leadership skills of managers. As Jim Foley, former Chief People Officer of Merkle,Inc once put it to me so clearly, "your team members don't quit the company, they quit you the manager."

With the plethora of resources available, having team members onsite allows managers to experiment with different management techniques. The fundamental attributes one has to demonstrate in other to succeed such as trust, care, nurturing, delegation, accountability, great attitude, transparency, maturity, flexibility, motivation are made much more feasible when in the same vicinity as the direct report. The hard reality is they are made more difficult as the cushion of proximity is removed. How do you demonstrate trust to someone who is on another location when you can't get the team in the office to trust you? How do you nurture a team member working from home when you are incapable of developing the talent sitting in the cube next to you? How are you able to motivate resources you can't personally interact with when you have failed to motivate the people performing inside the building where you stand?

Remote workers pull the veil off of managers' insecurities and often off of their shortcomings. If you are impatient in nature, but are able to contain it with people who work in your office, you will find it quite difficult to maintain that level of control when your resources are miles away and the only way you can interact with them is through virtual means.

With so much focus on technology in today's world, we sometimes forget that no number of computers and devices can make up for the lack of human skills. Non-technological, "old-fashioned" skills and practices that are essential for effective management. Businesses with remote workers need managers who have not only technological skills but also solid managerial skills.

If you are feeling uncomfortable at this point, brace yourself, for it is about to get worse before it gets better. Do not focus on just improving your ability to manage remote workers, but strive to become an overall better manager and account for the subtleties which apply to the people who do not work in the same location as you.

When dealing with telecommuters, managers sometimes forget the fundamentals of good management. Workers who are not in the office are dealing with the same issues their counterparts in the office are, with the added pressure of being by themselves without the social support of the tribe. It is easy for the manager to forget the coping mechanism that is offered by a group setting that is in the hive. You should] be aware that the number one complaint of off-site employees is a feeling of not being in the loop.

All of these problems can be solved simply by using sound business management practices in addition to recognizing and attending to the specific needs and concerns of the remote worker. Essential to doing this is to be aware of the common mistakes made by people in your situation. If you remain aware of these potential pitfalls, you are much more likely to avoid them altogether.

Not trusting the remote worker, and micromanaging
When dealing with the discomfort that comes with managing a team in a remote location, a manager might try to overcompensate for not having the employee under his/her supervision in the office, by micromanaging the remote employee and not trusting him/her. This is a destructive practice, as micromanaging and demonstrations of distrust will negatively affect the employee's confidence and initiative. Instead of micromanaging, the manager should ensure the lines of communication between

him/her and the employee are open and consistently used. People often fail to realize when they are micromanaging and attribute their overbearing presence to accountability. The manager must ensure the remote employee feels empowered to do their job with a certain degree of freedom. This is very important especially if you hire A Players and put them in the remote working situation. The type of individuals who excel in a telecommuting setting already spend a great deal of time evaluating themselves and understand the responsibility they ought to bear. Micromanaging them will undermine their ability to perform. The employee should be encouraged to feel a sense of investment and ownership with regard to the business and the project at hand.

The other extreme: Ignoring the remote worker

Another danger is the manager will, on purpose or not, ignore the remote workers under his/her supervision. Special care must be taken to ensure an "out of sight, out of mind" mentality does not take hold. Similarly to workers who are micromanaged and not trusted, workers who are ignored will feel discouraged and will lose their sense of investment in the company. These two extremes are highly destructive. Employees who are ignored will feel out of the loop, and are much less likely to take initiative and function with confidence and assurance. Lack of instruction and direction will likely lead to a fall in productivity, as time may be spent working on the wrong things or things the company considers a low priority.

Setting unrealistic deadlines

If the manager is not keeping track of what each employee is currently working on and what their current assignment deadlines are, it will be easy to overload them at the end. Lack of communication and losing track of employee assignments results in a situation where managers feel like in order to meet the company expectations, they have to resort to setting unrealistic deadlines. The "out of sight, out of mind" mentality that causes this situation to occur can lead to managers not demonstrating empathy towards their remote team. When you set unrealistic deadlines to telecommuters, you have to understand they will default to not eat and sleep and neglect other life objections until the work gets done. Unlike the workers in the office who can leave work at work, remote teams live in their work environment, so the temptation to overwork is heavy.

Not dealing with problems as they arise

The fact that remote employees are not seen as often in the office as other workers, can lead the manager to put off some problems as they arise. The temptation is to prioritize the items that are right in front of us, and get to the other issues later. Whether they have to do with technology, poor performance, quality of work, HR violations etc… deal with these concerns immediately so the team working away from the office gets a chance to collect feedback and readjust. If you do not communicate with the remote employee in a timely manner, the problem can become worse and issues can compound. In the end, this could result in your team member losing his/her job or quitting on you.

Be the anchor and cultivate consistency

Managers of remote workers can also make the mistake of not being consistent with remote employees. This can mean not being consistent in one's evaluation of an individual employee's performance, or not being consistent in expectations on project. With this type of behavior, you create a perception of bias and favoritism towards employees who are physically in the office. Even if you have previously established a certain level of trust with your team, you stand to undermine that trust if employees feel like you waver in your management approach to them. The simplest way to overcome this is by just being who you are as a manager and not trying to fake it with remote employees. Provide accurate and objective feedback and the level of discipline applied to people in the office is very similar to that of those you are not.

Avoid decision based solely on second-hand feedback

Managers of remote workers may be prone to not giving employees the chance to tell their side of the story when problems arise, such as complaints from co-workers, other managers, or clients/customers. Even if they are absolutely wrong, allow remote employees to offer their side of the story in every circumstance. It is easy to overlook giving the telecommuters a chance to defend themselves when they are not there in the office. This can inadvertently lead to feelings of alienation and unfair evaluations.

Not all resources are made equal.

With the new enthusiasm for remote employment, managers may forget that not all employees may be suited to work remotely. You will not always get a chance to conduct a full recruiting as portrayed in Chapter 3 where you have A-Players as part of the people who work from home. Show some flexibility when it comes to your team members performance levels. Allow for the resources to grow into the role and get out of the way of those who are already succeeding.

While remote employment can be very beneficial to both employers and employees, managers must avoid making mistakes that will compromise or negate the benefits of the arrangement. A good relationship between the manager and the resource is the key to your success within the organization.

_7_
ON-GOING OPERATIONS AND BEST PRACTICES

"People feel disrespected when they show up and others don't" —
Susan Scott

*"Operations keeps the lights on, strategy provides a light at the end of
the tunnel, but project management is the train engine that moves the
organization forward." - Joy Gumz*

Running a business with team members spread across
many geographical locations successfully requires a great
deal of flexibility and process management acumen. In
office management is often compared to spinning plates,
and when you add in remote workers, the righteous
comparison would be spinning plates in two adjacent
rooms between which you have to run back and forth.

There are many pitfalls that are unique to the
telecommuting environment which could be

underestimated unless clearly thought of and through especially when it comes to standard operating procedures. It is simply that managing remote workers is not an easy endeavor. If you are too busy, if the organization of your day is not your thing, or if your schedule is such that you cannot reliably keep meeting commitments and take on additional nurturing commitments for the sake of your team, don't go further. It won't work. Put this book down and best of luck to you.

If you are still reading, you need to remember, you are the remote employee's key link to the rest of your organization. He or she needs to be able to reliably count on you to provide them with the connection, the support, and the opportunities for growth that they need.

At Merkle Inc, Laurel Upton is a rising star who has set herself apart by her ability to deliver strong results on a variety of accounts while working with a variety of team members located in and out of the Pittsburgh office where she is based. As a manager of remote workers who oversees the performance of team members who are spread about and yet are required to work together consider the following considerations which she shared with me:

"When working with remote workers, finding the right balance of communication frequency is crucial. You want to keep people involved, but you also do not want to interrupt them. It's easy to frequently yell over to your co-worker who sits right next to you. However, calling someone who is not in the office at the same rate may not be received as well. It's really just about what works best for your team. There is no 'right' mix here. For us, having scheduled "touch-bases" helped reduce some of the one-off phone calls and meetings, and it helps our telecommuting team members stay focused with fewer interruptions."

She then went on to explain:

"Understanding that work hours/flows may be different in different locations is the other major factor to consider. For example, it's typical for workers in New York to start later and leave later in the day, compared to those in Pittsburgh, where many workers tend to arrive very early and also leave early. Therefore, even though these two offices are in the same locations, being flexible with each other schedule and sensitive to the preferences of the rest of our team is important to our success. We understand what our remote team's schedule is like (i.e. working until 6:30-7:00 pm), and they understand that the rest of us like to leave early, if possible!"

You see the complexity of running a team that is even located in the same time zone. So how do you succeed? How do you make it work?

Start by laying out the ground work
Whether you recruit or inherit a remote working team, start by meeting with the employees to explain the lay of the land. Be clear with the employee going into the arrangement that it's going to be challenging. Be open about what the challenges are going to be. Even for people who have had some experience working remotely, **The Remote Worker's Guide to Excellence** is an excellent resource to help start or improve the remote from home experience. At the onset of this relationship, make sure your team members have a realistic picture of what it is going to be like reporting to you from a different location whether it is another office or their home. This is not a preaching session but rather an exchange between two professionals about to embark on an operating journey.

This shall not just occur at the beginning of the relationship. For every new project, for every new strategy, and for every endeavor, meet with your remote team members and reach an operating agreement; determine up front what the employee will do to assure it works, and commit to what you will do.

Provide the resources needed to get the job done

When you have some employees who don't actually have to go to work in your office, it is not necessary for the company to supply them with a desk, parking and other items they would otherwise need. This is one of the biggest advantages, especially for small companies. It considerably reduces the capital required to run a business. These advantages should not become the expense of the telecommuters to do their job. Confirm that your team gets the hardware and software they will require in the field or at home to perform at their top level. Faulty equipment is one of the main frustrations shared with our research team. Frequently inquire about the state of the materials your remote team has been provided with and ensure they benefit from all the upgrades and improvements enjoyed by the people in the office. Resources go beyond equipment and software. If there are in-office team members that the telecommuter needs to interact with in order to get the job done, make the proper introductions and set the expectations to all team members both in and out of the building.

For your employees who are contractors, make sure they have provided themselves with the right materials. Take the time to conduct an audit of what they have available and ready to support them in this regard, though this may not be a conventional practice. The more you invest in your team members, the more you get in return. For example, it is common for companies not to provide healthcare for contractors, if your organization wants to attract and retain top talents, you should consider some kind of health saving plan which would help them meet medical needs should the issue arise.

Allow a trial period.

As mentioned earlier, telecommuting is not for everyone. Allow a trial period; for example 90 days, to substantiate if telecommuting arrangement makes the most sense for you and your employees. Since all companies are different, even a telecommuting veteran at another company, may find it challenging to operate in your company from a different location. Working with you as the manager may be a challenge to some remote workers who have successfully reported to other people. At the end of the trial period, you can either allow employees to continue telecommuting, make some adjustment on how they are to continue to work remotely, or require them to work in the office, depending on how well things went during that time.

Train telecommuters properly.

Telecommuters have unique knowledge needs for everything from how to log into the company network and set up teleconferences to how to communicate with a geographically dispersed team. The right training, or lack thereof, can mean the difference between success and contentment or failure and frustration.

Provide opportunities for in-person socialization.

Many telecommuters feel "out of the loop" when it comes to the goings-on in the office, and the folks in the office feel the same way about their telecommuting peers. We will review issues about engagement in an upcoming chapter, but understand that inviting your telecommuting employees to onsite social functions, whether at the home office or satellite locations, gives you a chance to get to know telecommuters as people and see the faces behind the screen.

Set up a structure for accountability.

People work harder and accomplish more when they feel accountable. A telecommuting arrangement should provide a solid structure for accountability, whether it involves weekly status reports or quarterly onsite one-on-one sessions. You have to find the rate that works for you and your remote workers.

Deliver on your commitments

Do what you said you would do. It sounds simple enough but telling a telecommuter, let me call you back and then proceeding not to do so, leaves someone in the field or at home by themselves worrying about why you did not call back instead of getting back to work. As part of your commitment to them, follow up to make sure the employee has all they need and that you both are on the same page.

_8_
BE AN AVAILABLE MANAGER

"There is nothing that harvests more of a feeling of empowerment than being of service to someone in need." Gillian Anderson

It is plain and simple. Your remote worker needs you. If you don't make the time for them, you are setting them up for failure. Whether they work from home, drive a truck, or operate in a different facility, they have the expectation that someone on the other side is listening and stand ready to help. How would you feel if you were an astronaut in space needed guidance or seeking direction, and when you call the control room, you are welcomed with silence. "Houston, we've got a problem" would be quickly replaced by "Houston is the problem."

In the overall need for the remote worker to be connected and engaged, the primary point of connection and engagement is the direct manager. Managers have plenty on their plates these days, and when it's a remote team they manage, they have to be adroit at juggling their time. Here are a few examples of what's required of them in order for them to succeed and make their team succeed.

Authority and the casual contact:

Managers who rise to a certain level of authority are chosen for their responsibilities because they are leaders: resourceful, charismatic, focused and, in particular, trusted with keeping team productivity high. They are gifted at building relationships, and although the natural inclination would be for managers to establish relatively rigid mechanisms that protect them from too much casual exposure to team members, one of the requirements of those relationships has to be to section off time for impromptu chats or calls made to be friendly with team members, see how they're doing and just for shooting the breeze. These spontaneous calls permit the worker to vent on some matter or other and, at the very least, to feel appreciated and part of something bigger than themselves.

Limits and off limits:

Of concern is how managers choose to structure communication schedules and channels between team members and themselves and, at the core, how much of their personal time to give to others and in what ways. Part of the time-management effort that governs the relation of a manager with remote workers is recognition, acceptance and respect for the fact that managers "have a life", and that it includes a family, work, a passionate hobby (reading, golf, etc.) and going out with friends. Therefore, concise processes and schedules have to be established.

Soft or hard tactics:

Managers choose different tactics in wielding their influence. Soft or hard tactics may be required, depending on whether they absolutely must have a result or they can leave the other person with some maneuvering room.

When it comes to sacrificing some privacy and managing their availability, their prime concern is the isolation factor of working from home and loneliness that one of their team members may be going through. Managers thus become a replacement for the entire office staff in more conventional office settings. If they're not available to listen to someone who's down and needing to talk, they may lose a valuable team member.

Tactical assertiveness:

When necessary, managers can switch from soft tactics to additional assertiveness and a harder posture. In fact, in their quest to influence team members, managers have at their disposal a slew of tactics from inspirational, consultation, rational and assertive to hard. In adopting the soft approach of having rules that can at times be broken, managers can set aside a period of the day when they are available not for a formal video conference, which would be the more conventional method for "meetings", but for one-on-one calls initiated by team members.

Be smart, not tough:

At the back of a manager's thinking invariably lurks the degree of strain he or she can put on a particular relationship –an easy line to cross. Of prime consideration in that context is the turnover factor, dreaded for its gobbling up of managerial time and resources. Time management becomes much easier once there is an understanding at the level of setting up communication priorities and mechanisms, good for most routine needs. Together with the caveat that people can make the occasional exception, this should be looked upon not as a detriment but as a series of disciplines that everyone can benefit from. Managers can thus also encourage team members to seek balance in their lives in part by enjoying their own version of "signing off" outside of work time.

Going abroad:

Today's managers are at times also asked to exert their influence internationally. With the ever-growing number of multinational corporations that have licensing arrangements and subsidiaries in far-off places, there is a great deal to be said for a manager trying to keep tabs over multiple work-at-home co-workers on different continents. Beyond overcoming all the other issues that often act as barriers to good team productivity, managers have to show they can rise above language, time zone and cultural hurdles and be able to keep someone in Tokyo or Hong Kong motivated. But even in cases like that, it is also important proper communication channels be set, including video conferencing and the broad use of Skype and similar services. Needless to say, Managers have to make themselves available in manners they would normally prefer to avoid, such as middle of the night and weekend calls for what a team member might perceive as being critical matter.

Command-style methods:

With the rise of international virtual teams like that, managers who may never have met these distant workers and who may not have official authority over them, have had to sharpen their skills in the fields of building rapports, influencing others, persuading, negotiating, networking, using "command-style" methods to assert their leadership and preempt obstacles. On the softer side is a human being, sitting at his or her home thousands of miles away, who has more or less the same needs as the nearby worker, as remote as they are from the camaraderie that warms relations between staff members at the head office.

Catching a small fire before it becomes big:

Great managers are great because they're good at keeping the spirits high amidst their ranks. When morale is in the dumps, up goes employee turnover and down goes the team's overall productivity. Even when a team is purring efficiently, this is never far from a manager's mind. In addition, great managers intuitively sense when something is not right with one or more team members. By making themselves instantly available, this mindfulness enables a manager to catch a small fire before it becomes big.

Scouting for talent:

Like sports scouts, managers may also attempt to locate and recruit new individuals. Being in charge of a remote workforce allows them the luxury of finding people with precisely the talent and strengths needed not just from nearby places but from distant places as well. When that happens, they have to provide time in spades for mentoring, coaching, taking the new recruit to the head office, and seeing them through their formal training. Once on the job, they have to hold the new hire's hands through the initial post-training period.

To sum up, the best advice to managers and would-be team leaders is to bring out your personality and let it flourish, the one that radiates with self-compassion and empathy for others. Communication arrangements are fine, and so are policies and procedures, but at the end of the day your team members will work extra hard if they view you as a natural leader.

_9_
WHAT IS THE BIG DEAL ABOUT ENGAGEMENT?

"No man is an island, entire of itself; each is a piece of the continent, a part of the main" - John Donne

At many instances so far in this book, we have referred to "engagement" as being a crucial element to the success of both the remote worker and their manager. As the manager you need to understand that remote teams will be challenged by the fact that, despite modern technologies, they will find it difficult to be fully integrated in the team dynamic. Most of the activities that create a stellar team dynamic are often unplanned. Grabbing lunch together, stopping by the water cooler, brainstorming, sharing jokes, and other things that can make the work place more integrated require physical presence. Engagement is the primary reason put forward by Yahoo! in order to send the remote workers packing. Though the solution is misguided, it does not invalidate the concerns it is trying to address. Telecommuters are often not very immersed in office politics; therefore they may not know how to navigate the political minefields and classify the unwritten rules of your organization.

Worker engagement has been aptly defined as maximum contribution to produce optimal reward and fulfillment. Many companies still don't have adequate guidance for work-from-home employees. They tend to leave things in the hands of managers. The task of coming up with a flexible yet productive work environment that does the job is thus left, for the most part, to you the team leaders.

With that in mind, managers are entrusted with one of their most taxing assignments which is also the hardest to keep track of: developing a culture of engagement in which everyone has a role and feels part of the whole. It is taxing because of its seesawing action between throwing their arms up in exasperation one day and feeling exalted the next.

Leaders of remote teams are nothing short of heroes
Managers have to be temperamentally stable and not easily derailed. You have to be well suited to be both disciplinarian and sociable, available yet not over-exposed, stern yet logical, deliberate yet spontaneous and, most significantly, regimented yet flexible.

You must display leadership qualities that include high moral values, great listening skills, reliable judgment, clarity of thought and speech, transparency, and a sensory capacity that enables you to become aware of issues before they happen. Yours is the task of building trusting relationships and intuitively understanding each person's engagement drivers and talents.

A critical task is that of assimilating remote workers as they join the group and keeping them in the fold thereafter. It is also the surest way to achieve success in this arena as once the telecommuter is disconnected, it is an herculean task to bring them back in the fold.

10 Guidelines for assimilating new team members:

1.Facilitate the integration of newcomers to the group and encourage ongoing communications with the rest of the team via video conferencing as well as impromptu one-on-one Skype conversations between them.

2.Facilitate the integration of team members with department heads and co-workers at HQ and ensure that direct communications are encouraged and channels kept open.

3.Send out circulars within your division -or higher still- introducing newcomers and highlighting the talent and experience they bring along and the role you expect them to play in reinforcing the team.

4.Accompany team members on training and conferencing visits to HQ and ensure that they are given adequate attention and assistance.

5.Ensure that HR staff at HQ, or the manager's direct supervisor, consider remote workers in the same light as office workers when it comes to awards, commemorations, celebrations. Also include them in publications such as the company directory.

6.Get the collaboration of relevant executives and supervisors to keep the remote worker connected with what is transpiring at the level of clients, new products, new schemes in the offing.

7.Help team members to remain engaged and not to get disconnected because of lack of sufficient attention and time given them. Use out-of-the-box thinking to make them feel that they own a piece of the culture or bond that reigns within the team.

8.Don't miss an opportunity to get each team member to be physically in contact with other team members (birthdays, achievement awards, etc.)

9.Have short surveys on a regular basis to accurately establish the engagement level of each of the team members.

10. Ensure that all team members accept and take ownership in the authority of the engagement measuring metrics that is in practice.

How do you go about motivating virtual workers?

Engagement is a two-way practice. Both the manager and the telecommuters bear the responsibility to be as engaged as necessary for the success of the organization. The greatest issues standing in the way of the remote worker to be pro-active in their engagement endeavor is when they are not feeling motivated and/or supported by you the manager. The lack of the motivation and support will create many inefficiencies in the work flow and affect more than just the team member's ability to be engaged.

How can you know if a telecommuter is productive?

Formats, goals and bottom lines are necessary, but it's the culture and the manager's character and leadership that drive the team's productivity.

How do you ensure that no worker is left behind?

By dedicating themselves to building efficient communication systems, technology and other forms of support, and by advertising their availability at suitable times and in suitable ways.

Is there a solid ground for team communication?

Acknowledge the 24/7 setting that the team works in, where individuals work when and where they want; facilitate and promote communications via instant messaging, file sharing and video conferencing. Be prepared to lay out sufficient resources to remain up to date on the latest technology when it supports technology and makes sense for your team. Be the super coach when it comes to training team members on the best ways to communicate.

How do you keep tabs over team members?

Through regular short understandable employee engagement surveys that everyone buys into and by ensuring that performance reviews are based on team goals and project results, and not by any calendar triggers.

How do managers avoid employee turnover?

By having an intuitive feeling about who is in need of additional support and providing that support, and by being a proactive scout and keeping an eye out for new talent to plug away at the team's weakness.

How to augment senior level engagement?

The manager is too busy to act as mentor to every team member, thus the thing to do is to assign another team member to help a new recruit. That mentor's task then is to be more available to the newcomer and help them through cultural barriers, current policies and procedures and the communication routines that team members follow.

Encourage your coworkers to help you in keeping your team members engaged and feeling that they belong in the bigger picture. Share with your team members how most team achievements end up at your supervisor's desk, and that the supervisor will know that the good work came courtesy of the team. Alexis Sanders, a Search Specialist at Merkle Inc., works with a mix team of professionals. Some work in different offices, and some work from home. She shared with me the importance of intentional communication.

"Being remote makes communication much harder. You miss out on the Monday morning coffee machine chats, the lunch outings, and the evening Happy Hours. You unintentionally know much less about your teammates, than you would if you sat two cubicles down. There are no social cues, only your voice and your writing. One quickly finds that "thank you" becomes the most important word in your vocabulary. A simple "thank you" or "you rock" can show your teammates that they are appreciated for the amazing work they're doing."

_10_
GROWTH AND CAREER DEVELOPMENT

"Management is doing things right; leadership is doing the right things." - Peter Drucker

For your team, one of your main responsibilities is facilitating a promising path for growth. Career growth and development is challenging (and vital) for any employee. Remote employees face significant additional obstacles in this journey. They rarely or never have the opportunity to interact and meet in person with their co-workers and employers, and therefore it is very difficult for the organization to gauge the employees' unique strengths and abilities and think about where and how those qualities would be most effectively applied in the organization. As a result, it is important for employers with remote employees to take an active interest in ensuring that their workers have real opportunities to clearly demonstrate their strengths and areas of potential.

Regular employee performance feedback can be a very useful tool in facilitating consistent awareness. These reports can be weekly or bi-weekly and should summarize the work the employee has completed, the obstacles he or she has faced and overcome, and any questions he or she may have. It can be very useful to provide a template for this report, to ensure that the employees do not forget to address any one subject area. When employees are assigned specific projects, it is advisable to also require project progress reports to be written and submitted.

It is well known that sending employees for extra training is a quite common workplace practice. However, it seems to a bit less common in remote employment. It would be a good idea to change this. The employer should seek to show their employees that they have real faith in their ability to progress in their chosen careers, and a wonderful way to do this is to pay for additional training.

Open and frequent communication is absolutely essential. A practice that may be useful in allowing remote employees to interact with their co-workers is to assign tasks involving some measure of internet communication between them. Online staff meetings, staff message boards, and opportunities for chat are also very useful. The use of such tools will help remote workers stay in the loop, and therefore feel more confident. Employers who employ both traditional and remote employees sometimes forget the needs of the remote workers. Unfortunately, the "out of sight, out of mind" effect sometimes comes into play.

The aforementioned online staff message boards can be an invaluable tool in ensuring remote employees feel in the loop and connected to their co-workers and employer. They can be useful even if the employer has a relatively low number of remote employees in comparison to their on-site workers. Encourage both groups of workers can post on the board.

If staff meetings in person are not practical, online staff meetings can be facilitated through videoconferencing. It is also a good idea for employers to publish a newsletter periodically. This could be sent out by email, and "snail mail" as well, if desired. Additionally, all open and opening job positions and promotion opportunities should be posted online, to ensure that remote employees can see and consider them.

It must be remembered that certain career tracks simply do not lend themselves to working remotely. These include professions and positions that intrinsically require direct, in-person interaction with clients, customers, or, in the case of medical professionals, patients, and "hands on" work. Examples of the many jobs that are not suitable for remote employment include positions such as doctor, nurse, daycare worker, landscaper, plumber, cashier, and electrician. There are many positions, however, that can accommodate a combination of both on-site work and remote work. Examples of these include lawyer, accountant, consultant, and numerous other professional occupations.

Performance Feedback for Remote Employees

Essential to the career growth process is the carrying out of meaningful, clear, and helpful performance reviews. If workers are not kept aware of their employers' assessment of, and opinions about, their job performance, they cannot work to specifically improve their performance. If they have an accurate idea of how they have been, and are being, assessed, they can create targeted plans for improvement. The employer can also assist the remote worker with writing an action plan to guarantee progress.

Performance reviews do not have to be in person, unless there needs to be a discussion regarding issues which could jeopardize the remote employee's job. Such meetings should be in person, if possible, unless all work communication has been by another method throughout the employee's tenure (for example, by phone), and in person meetings are extremely unusual. You should keep consistent the methods of communication and not ask employees to travel to your location, if you typically communicate via phone or teleconference, if the topic is termination. If an in-person meeting is not possible otherwise, videoconferencing might be a good alternative.

There are several easily accessible online options for videoconferencing. In addition to these venues and applications, the employer needs to verify they have all the required equipment, and to ensure that the employee has a chance to acquire the equipment they need, as well. Depending on the exact nature of the employment agreement, the employer might be required to buy the equipment the employee needs for videoconferencing.

Regardless of any obstacles that must be overcome in its pursuit, career growth and development should be given intense attention, by remote employees and employers alike.

_11_
BE A MOTIVATOR AND A CHEERLEADER

"In everyone's life, at some time, our inner fire goes out. It is then burst into flame by an encounter with another human being. We should all be thankful for those people who rekindle the inner spirit."
— *Albert Schweitzer*

"In motivating people, you've got to engage their minds and their hearts. It is good business to have an employee feel part of the entire effort . . . ; I motivate people, I hope, by example—and perhaps by excitement, by having provocative ideas to make others feel involved."
— *Rupert Murdoch*

What are the things that contribute towards boosting the results of your workers? Is it the passion he has for the work or is it the pay check she gets that counts? Employers are often tempted to think that mere financial compensation is enough to reward employees. The reality is that though financial compensation goes a long way, team members are not just people whom you are compensating for a service rendered. Money is not a long-term motivator, for all. It is true that employees do love a good check, who doesn't love a check anyway? However they also expect that check. It is part of the basic agreement made when they accept working for you. If they perform well, they will get paid accordingly. Jim Foley shared with me that *"the best rewards for outstanding work comes from the heart, not the payroll department."*

When I was working as a remote employee for IMPAQT, a Search Agency based out Pittsburgh, I had to take a day off to be sworn in as a US citizen. It was not a work related activity, but for me it was one of my proudest moments. I was embracing this land to be my country. I was shifting my allegiance from the country that has seen me come into this world in favor of the country that has become my home. I came home after all was done, and on my front door, was a giant box with an overnight delivery label. I thought to myself that it must be very important. I rushed the package inside and proceeded to open it. Inside was an Apple Pie on ice, with a card that from my leaders, congratulating me on this achievement. The joy that filled my heart was indescribable. A few weeks later, I was having a rough day delivering on a project. I felt really challenged. I reminded myself of the degree of care that was demonstrated towards me, the memory motivated to perform even better, not because I was asked to, but because I was grateful.

According to Kenneth Kovach, you have to make sure that you ask yourself 10 key questions in order to create a motivational environment for your team members. These questions are relevant whether or not your team members are in the office are remote.

1. Do you personally thank remotes when they do well?

2. Do you give timely and specific feedback?
3. Do you make time to listen to your telecommuters?
4. Do you instill a dynamic that is open, trusting, and fun?
5. Do you encourage and reward innovation?
6. Do you share information regularly?
7. Do you involve your team in decisions affecting them?
8. Do you give ownership to your team regarding their work ?
9. Do you give your team the opportunity to succeed?
10. Do you reward the team based on their performance?

By honestly answering these questions it will allow you to fully grasp the components needed to create a successful workplace for your team members. People who work from home or in remote locations do not get the ability to high-five other. It does not take much to show appreciation to team members, but the effect of a little effort would go a long way in boosting the morale of the team.

In the <u>Remote Worker's Guide to Excellence</u>, we explore the notion that the remote worker is ultimately responsible for their surround sound. It is important that you, as the manager, play an active role in the building and maintaining of that surround sound.

> *"Awards are a great way to motivate from a-far... or just giving credit where credit is due as well as praising team members in front of senior management and our clients. Remote team members can be overlooked since they aren't physically seen. Managers and peers should make announcements in front of the company showcasing the remote team member's work, if applicable."* - Laurel Upton

By being a voice that shares the successes of your remote team members, serve as an amplification tool in the effort to improve upon their surround sound. It is important to realize that being the number one cheerleader of your remote workforce is a key asset which enhances the success the team and that of your business. Being a cheerleader and a motivator does not mean that you sugarcoat things or that you only focus on the positive. You must deliver honest, candid, and sincere feedback.

12

HOW DO YOU KNOW IF YOU ARE SUCCEEDING OR FAILING?

You now have all the tools, materials and strategies needed to excel at managing telecommuters. Understanding the performance signals of your remote employees is important, but more crucial is having a great pulse on your own performance as a manager. A great manager takes responsibility for the performance of his people, and an even better manager understands that where she goes, so does the team she manages. There are proven signs that, if aware of them, will help you understand whether or not you are heading in the right direction. The earliest you identify issues to solve, the quicker you can make the necessary adjustments for the sake of your team members and that of your organization.

When it is working...
The greatest point of success in managing remote workers is in getting the same feedback from the people in the office as you get from the people who are not. When you

ask the remote employee - as you do other employees - what is working and what isn't, if the answers are similar, you have just established that your in-house culture is carried through to the rest of the organization. This pauses a great deal of challenges. If you fix the issues in the office, you will have to make sure that the solutions put into place are reverberated and felt among your remote employees.

In my training seminars, you will hear me talk over and over again about the importance of the surround sound. The establishment of a solid surround sound is one of the most difficult things to do in an office environment. A surround sound is the perception of you that people who do not work directly with you have of you and of your performance level. Getting a bad reputation or no reputation at all is quite easy. Considering how hard it is to do when you are already in the office, now imagine how hard that must be when you are a remote employee. Consider it there for a great sign of success when you hear a lot of positives about the remote employee's work contributions from the team and beyond.

An extension of the previous point is a phenomenon that is quite subtle and often missed by many managers. It is the existence of a successful team dynamic within the team reporting into you regardless of whether the team member is remote. You know that you are doing the right thing by your remote when others engage the employee as if he or she were right there in the room. The team members are at ease with you and with others within the organization.

When your remote team members are successful, you will start to notice a positive shift in their surround sound around the organization. Peers share with you ways they have been instrumental for the success of the team, and you get requests from other teams to get an opportunity to consult/work/talk with your telecommuters.

When it is not working....

Most of the red flags evolve around engagement. When we feel disconnected with the remote team members on your team, you need to take measures to correct your current course. If like the folks at Yahoo!, you are starting to see that the contribution made by the telecommuters are not as important as that made by the team members which are on-location. With the depreciation of the value of their contribution also comes the drop in their participation level which ramps up rapidly when you addressed head on.

All employees complain. Remote workers are however aware of the privilege they have working from home, so they tend of complain less. Therefore an increase in the amount of complaining and negativity from a team member who works remotely is a clear indication that you are failing as a manager. Employees send signals that you should be able to read by now whether they are in the office or not. Their level of participation is proportional to the perceived worth they have of what they are doing. When your telecommuters stop attending or participating in team meetings, you must immediately reevaluation your performance and identified the triggers. Performance improvement policies could be engaged at that time, but a look in the mirror before charging to fix things would do you and your team a great deal of favor.

When the volume of their surround sound is low across the organization, it means that you have failed to promote your team members' contribution, or you have not equipped your team with the ability to share and celebrate their wins. Therefore, when peers fail to mention the contribution of your remote workers or only share with you complaints and negative feedback about your telecommuters, you need to take decisive measures to rectify the course and go make sure you are a good motivator and a cheerleader for your team.

It is important when evaluating your performance level with remote workers, you trust your managerial instinct. If you feel something is out of sync and that there seems to have been a shift, you should be concerned. There is wisdom in maintaining the course for consistency, but understand that *"just because you're paranoid doesn't mean they aren't after you"* — Joseph Heller. If you suspect that there could be a problem, explore and find out whether or not you were mistaken. At the very least, you would have gotten an opportunity to check on the pulse of your team members, but at best you would have identified a problem early enough in the funnel that you would have been able to solve before it actually becomes a real issue. Never invalidate or brush off your feelings in this situation, but rather assess them. If they are unfounded, move; if they are not, take action to rectify course.

_13_
WISDOM, KNOWLEDGE AND UNDERSTANDING

In the Torah as well as in the Christian Old Testament, a story appears two separate times. It is an account of an interaction between King Solomon and his God (2 Chronicles 1,1 Kings 3, (Pesiḳ. R. 14 [ed. Friedmann, p. 59a, b]; Num. R. xix. 3; Eccl. R. vii. 23; Midr. Mishle i. 1, xv. 29).

> God appeared to Solomon and said to him, "Ask for whatever you want me to give you."

> Solomon answered "God, you have shown great kindness to David, my father, and have made me king in his place. Now, Lord God, let your promise to my father David be confirmed, for you have made me king over a people who are as numerous as the dust of the earth. Give me wisdom and knowledge, that I may lead this people, for who is able to govern this great people of yours?"

God said to Solomon, "Since this is your heart's desire and you have not asked for wealth, possessions or honor, nor for the death of your enemies, and since you have not asked for a long life but for wisdom and knowledge to govern my people over whom I have made you king, therefore wisdom and knowledge will be given you. And I will also give you wealth, possessions and honor, such as no king who was before you ever had and none after you will have."

If you are put in a situation where three things can be bestowed upon you to lead remote workers, do indeed ask for Wisdom, Knowledge, and Understanding. If you are not put in that situation to mystically receive them, then work your butt off to make sure you acquire and exercise them. Managing a remote team is not a faint exercise. Yours is a virtual leadership role in which you are always looking out for the company's wellbeing as well as that of your team members. Working on this dual mission requires subtle ways to remind your colleagues and supervisors at the office that you have your team members' best interests at heart. By frequently reminding your team members that the team needs to look out for the company, since you and the company look out for them in return. You cannot just say these things, you have to demonstrate them.

Being a manager of a remote worker is an honorable and challenging responsibility that comes with a lot of pitfalls, many of which you don't have control over. The way to success is to make sure you deliver excellence in the areas you do have control over. The formula to achieve this is quite simple.

• You must start by observing the real life examples of the people around you and learn from their successes and their mistakes. In doing so, remember that other companies which have failed are not the norm but the exception not to follow. You can make this work.

- To make it work you start by hiring the right resources to do the job that you require to be performed by telecommuters. In your onboarding and every day thereafter, assure you maintain your integrity as a leader and that you are seen as a person of character.

- Being a leader of character starts by understanding and acknowledging the challenges that come with leading a team of people who are not in your physical vicinity. Be honest about your own ability to face those challenges. Create a plan based on that knowledge and execute on that plan.

- In this execution, be available and engage your team. Keep a keen eye on the development and growth of your resources and be their number one fan.

- Being a cheerleader of your team members does not absolve you of the responsibility to be a fair judge and constructively critical of their progress. Be aware of the indicators and red flags which you would use to gauge if you are succeeding or failing.

Remember your team is a reflection of your ability to lead and manage. If your team fails, it means that you are failing and when they succeed, you are too. By embracing the concepts and applying the practical elements contained in this book, you will achieve the blessed calling of managing remote workers.

As you grow in your ability to excel in how to manage remote workers, always exercise good judgment in interpreting the goals at hand and how to communicate them to your team in a way that empowers them in good and bad times by taking actions and making decisions with a great deal of regard to the application of your own acquired experience (wisdom). Make sure to collect facts and information about what is known of the project or situation you are about to face (knowledge). Never miss the intended meaning/goal/significance of what your team is working on and be sympathetically aware of the character and nature of both your team, clients, and all stakeholders your decisions impact (wisdom).

Best of luck to you and God bless!

Eryck Komlavi Dzotsi

REFERENCES

- What Marissa Mayer Doesn't Get About Telecommuting http://eryckdzotsi.com/what-marissa-mayer-doesnt-get-about-telecommuting/

- Yahoo! Internal Memo http://allthingsd.com/20130222/physically-together-heres-the-internal-yahoo-no-work-from-home-memo-which-extends-beyond-remote-workers/

- Reuters Reports on Aetna http://www.reuters.com/article/2013/03/01/us-yahoo-telecommuting-aetna-idUSBRE92006820130301

- Redefining Employee Satisfaction: Business Performance, Employee Fulfillment, and Leadership Practices http://www.ekser.com.tr/images/eBulten/Redefining%20Employee%20Satisfaction.pdf

- Kovach, Kenneth. (1999). Employee motivation: Addressing a crucial factor in your organization's performance. Human Resource Development. Ann Arbor, MI: University of Michigan Press.

ABOUT THE AUTHOR

Eryck Dzotsi (@erycked - www.eryckdzotsi.com) is an innovative Search Marketing Professional with 10 years of enterprise digital marketing expertise, with a solid track record of helping individuals and organizations beat their competition. He has developed and implemented strategies for businesses, non-profit organizations, and politicians around the world. His versatility has earned him the nickname of Marketing Renaissance Man by his clients. He can make even the most complex issues palatable for everyone from executives to administrative support staff members.

Eryck Komlavi Dzotsi is an experienced telecommuter who has lent his expertise to leading organizations in their respective industries and fields, including Merkle, the Embanet-Compass Group, Turnstile Publishing Company, Usbid.com, and ZoukStation.

As a serial entrepreneur, he has also been instrumental to the success of companies such as Squad, Qomlavy Networks, 321Agency, MJM Tropical, Zion Capital Investments. Eryck has a Bachelor of Science degree in both Management Information Systems and Business Administration from the Florida Institute of Technology.

Born in the Republic of Togo, Eryck lived in many countries among which France, Ivory Coast, Ghana, and Benin prior to immigrating to the United States. Eryck is a man of Faith who is heavily involved in helping his community. He serves in different organizations in his hometown of Melbourne, FL where he volunteers in ministries with focus on coaching sports and serving the poor, the sick, the homeless, the youth and the elderly.

Made in the USA
Lexington, KY
03 June 2015